NITROGEN

A TRUE BOOK®

by
Salvatore Tocci

Children's Press®
A Division of Scholastic Inc.

New York Toronto London Auckland Sydney
Mexico City New Delhi Hong Kong
Danbury, Connecticut

Nitrogen gas is commonly used to inflate the tires on race cars.

Reading Consultant
Julia McKenzie Munemo, EdM
New York, New York

Science Consultant
John A. Benner
Austin, Texas

The photo on the cover shows liquid nitrogen. The photo on the title page shows lightning, which can affect the nitrogen in the air.

The author and the publisher are not responsible for injuries or accidents that occur during or from any experiments. Experiments should be conducted in the presence of or with the help of an adult. Any instructions of the experiments that require the use of sharp, hot, or other unsafe items should be conducted by or with the help of an adult.

Library of Congress Cataloging-in-Publication Data

Tocci, Salvatore.
    Nitrogen / by Salvatore Tocci.
        p. cm. — (A true book)
    Includes bibliographical references and index.
    Contents: How deep can you dive?—What is nitrogen?—Why is nitrogen so important?—When is nitrogen dangerous?
    ISBN 0-516-22831-5 (lib. bdg.)   0-516-27850-9 (pbk.)
    1. Nitrogen—Juvenile literature. [1. Nitrogen.] I. Title. II. Series.
QD181.N1T66 2004
546'.711—dc22   2003016420

CHILDREN'S PRESS, and A TRUE BOOK™, and associated logos are trademarks and or registered trademarks of Scholastic Library Publishing. SCHOLASTIC and associated logos are trademarks and or registered trademarks of Scholastic Inc.

1 2 3 4 5 6 7 8 9 10 R 13 12 11 10 0

0 1021 0178321 9

Contents

How Deep Can You Dive?   5

What Is Nitrogen?   11

Why Is Nitrogen So Important?   22

When Is Nitrogen Dangerous?   31

Fun Facts About Nitrogen   42

To Find Out More   44

Important Words   46

Index   47

Meet the Author   48

How Deep Can You Dive?

Have you ever swum deep underwater? If you have, then you may have felt the water pressing against your eardrums. You can feel this pressure by diving down just a few feet below the water's surface. The deeper you go, the more pressure you will feel pushing against your eardrums.

Scuba divers swim very deep underwater. While swimming underwater, a diver breathes air from a tank. Air is made up of invisible gases. The air in a diver's tank contains the same gases that are in the air we breathe on land. However, the air in a scuba tank is compressed. This

This diver is breathing compressed air from a tank.

means that the gases in the tank are under a much higher pressure than they are on land.

The high pressure makes it possible for the diver to breathe while swimming in deep water. The pressure forces the gases out of the tank, into the diver's lungs, and then into his or her bloodstream. As long as the diver remains in deep water, the gases will stay in his or her blood. However, the gases come back out of the blood as the diver rises to the surface.

A diver who has spent some time deep underwater must come to the surface very slowly. This allows the gases to come out of the blood slowly and safely. If the diver rises too quickly to the surface, the gases come out of the blood too quickly and form bubbles. These gas bubbles collect in the body and cause severe pain. This condition is commonly known as "the bends." The gas that causes the bends is nitrogen.

What Is Nitrogen?

Nitrogen is an element. An **element** is the building block of matter. **Matter** is the stuff or material that makes up everything in the universe. This book, the chair you are sitting on, and even your body are all made of matter.

There are millions of different kinds of matter. However, there are just a few more than one hundred different elements. How can so many different kinds of matter be made up of so few elements? Think about the English language. Just twenty-six letters can be arranged to make up all the words in the language. Likewise, the approximately one hundred different elements can be combined in

Nitrogen is the fifth most abundant element in the universe.

different ways to make up all the kinds of matter in the universe.

Nitrogen was discovered in 1772 during a simple experiment. Scientists placed a burning candle inside a jar filled with air. They noticed that the flame went out. At that time, scientists knew that nothing burns without oxygen. The scientists concluded that the flame went out because there was no more oxygen left inside the jar.

Substances burn only
when oxygen is present.

However, the scientists knew that there was still plenty of air left inside the jar. They concluded that air must contain another gas besides oxygen. This other gas was first called "burnt air" and was later named nitrogen. Besides a name, each element has a symbol. The symbol for nitrogen is N, which comes from the first letter of its name.

Nitrogen gas has no color, odor, or taste. Nitrogen gas also makes up almost 80 percent of the air we breathe. Both plants and animals need nitrogen to live. Unfortunately, living things cannot use the nitrogen gas that is in the air. The nitrogen gas must first be changed into a substance that plants and animals can use. This job is carried out by tiny organisms that live on the

The swellings on these roots are groups of bacteria that change nitrogen into a substance animals and plants can use.

roots of certain plants. These tiny living things are called **bacteria**. Bacteria are part of a process called the **nitrogen cycle**. The nitrogen cycle is nature's way of recycling nitrogen.

Bacteria change nitrogen into a compound. A **compound** is a substance that is made from the combination of two or more different elements. Bacteria combine nitrogen with

The nitrogen cycle involves
air, land, plants, and animals.

other elements to make compounds that plants can absorb
from the soil. In turn, animals
get the nitrogen they need by
eating plants and other animals
that have eaten plants. When
plants and animals die, the
nitrogen is eventually released
back into the air.

Why Is Nitrogen So Important?

All living things need nitrogen. Nitrogen is used by living things to make compounds they need to survive. For example, nitrogen is used to make **proteins**. Proteins help build certain parts of our bodies, such as muscles. Proteins

The process of getting the energy you need to play involves a compound that contains nitrogen.

also play an important role in controlling what happens in our bodies. One such protein is insulin. Insulin controls the level of sugar that is in the blood. Our bodies turn sugar into energy.

You read that bacteria use nitrogen to make compounds that plants can use. One compound that bacteria make from nitrogen is ammonia. Bacteria are not the only source of ammonia. Factories also use nitrogen to make huge amounts of ammonia. The ammonia is

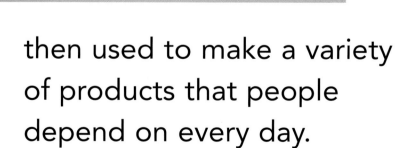

Ammonia is mixed
with water to make
a liquid that is used
to clean grease.

CLEAR
AMMONIA

NET 64 FL OZ (2 QTS) 1.89 L

then used to make a variety
of products that people
depend on every day.

Writing Secret Messages

Mix equal parts of water and clear ammonia. Dip a cotton swab in the diluted ammonia. Use the swab to write your name on a piece of white paper. Ask an adult to help you boil some chopped-up red cabbage in water. After it cools, pour the colored liquid into a bowl or spray bottle. Spray the liquid onto the paper where you wrote your name. Your name should appear in green. Experiment with different kinds of paper to see which is best for writing secret messages.

Fertilizer provides plants with the nitrogen they need to grow.

Most ammonia is used to make fertilizers. Fertilizers are added to the soil to provide more nitrogen to help plants grow. Without fertilizers, farmers could not grow as many crops as they do. The amount of nitrogen in a fertilizer is printed on the label. The label contains a series of three numbers, such as 5-10-5. These numbers tell you the percent of three elements that are in the fertilizer. The first number shows how much nitrogen is present. In this case, the fertilizer contains 5 percent nitrogen.

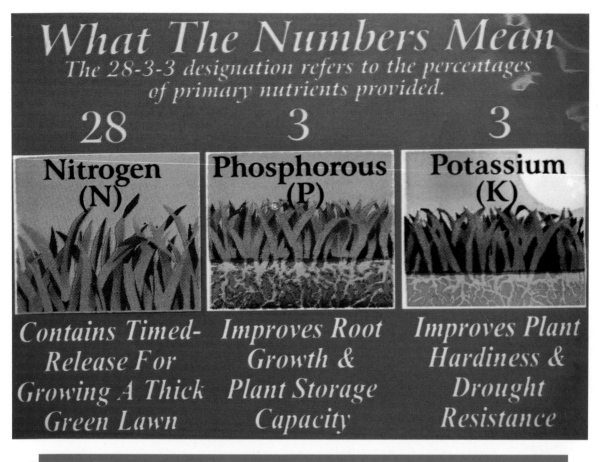

What The Numbers Mean

The 28-3-3 designation refers to the percentages of primary nutrients provided.

28	3	3
Nitrogen (N)	**Phosphorous (P)**	**Potassium (K)**
Contains Timed-Release For Growing A Thick Green Lawn	Improves Root Growth & Plant Storage Capacity	Improves Plant Hardiness & Drought Resistance

Fertilizers are added to the soil to provide more nitrogen to help plants grow. Each bag of fertilizer has three numbers listed. The first number is the percentage of nitrogen in the fertilizer. The second and third numbers tell how much phosphorus and potassium, both elements, are in the fertilizer.

Besides fertilizers, ammonia is used to make fibers for clothing, plastics, vitamins, and medicines. Ammonia is also used to make rocket fuel and "smelling salts" for waking up people who have fainted.

When Is Nitrogen Dangerous?

Although nitrogen is used to make compounds that are very useful, it is also used to make compounds that can cause a lot of damage. For example, compounds that contain nitrogen are used to make explosives. The use of nitrogen to make explosives played an important role in world history.

During the 1910s, World War I was being fought in Europe. On one side were Germany and its allies. On the other side were the United States and its allies, including England and France. Both sides sought out the world's richest source of nitrogen, which is a compound called sodium nitrate that can be used to make explosives. This source was in Chile. For thousands of years, large numbers of seabirds had nested along the coast of Chile. The solid droppings from these birds had built up into huge piles that were several feet high and several miles long. These piles were rich in sodium nitrate.

PERU

BOLIVIA

Lake Titicaca

Volcano Islugo

Atacama Desert

Loa

COASTAL RANGE

Volcano Llullaillaco

Nevado Ojos
del Salado

ARGENTINA

CHILE

CORDILLERA DE LOS ANDES

Valparaíso

Santiago

Concepción

Bío-Bío

ANDES DE PATAGONIA

ATLANTIC
OCEAN

Lake Gen. Carrera

At one time, Chile
was the richest
source of a nitrogen
compound needed
to make explosives.

Strait of Magellan

PACIFIC
OCEAN

Cape Horn

England and France quickly set up a blockade to prevent German ships from reaching Chile. Without a supply of sodium nitrate to make its explosives, Germany would be forced to surrender. However, German scientists developed a way to change nitrogen gas into ammonia. Like sodium nitrate, ammonia can be used to make explosives. German industries were soon making huge quantities of ammonia. As a result, Germany had enough explosives to allow World War I to continue until 1918. If the German scientists had not developed a way to make ammonia, the war would have ended much sooner.

Ammonia was used to make explosives even before World War I. The most powerful explosive was a nitrogen compound called nitroglycerin. Nitroglycerin is a liquid that

Nitrogen was an important ingredient in the explosives used during World War I.

explodes very easily. In 1867, Alfred Nobel invented a way to turn the dangerous liquid into a paste that did not explode as easily. He called his new invention dynamite. Nobel made a fortune by making and selling dynamite. Upon his death in 1896, he left his fortune to establish the Nobel Prizes, which are still awarded to experts in several subjects today.

Alfred Nobel believed that his discovery would lead to world peace. He thought people would fear the terrible destruction that dynamite could cause.

Making Smog

Another dangerous nitrogen compound is found in the smog that causes air pollution. You can make your own smog. Use a piece of aluminum foil to make a cover for a wide glass jar. Gently press down on the foil. Remove the foil. Pour some water into the jar, swish it around, and then pour it down a sink.

Have an adult use a match to light a small piece of paper on fire and drop it into the jar. Quickly cover the jar with the foil. Then quickly place some ice cubes on top of the foil. You should see smog form inside the jar. Be sure to open the jar outside to get rid of your smog.

Fun Facts About Nitrogen

- To make ammonia, nitrogen must be kept under a pressure that is equal to that found 1 1/4 miles (2 kilometers) below sea level.

- Nitrogen turns into a liquid at −320 degrees Fahrenheit (−196 degrees Celsius). A banana placed in liquid nitrogen will get so hard that it can be used to hammer a nail into a wall.

- Besides bacteria, lightning can also change nitrogen into a compound that plants can absorb. About 10 million tons of this compound are made every year on Earth by lightning.

- Nitrogen gas is commonly used to inflate the tires on airplanes and race cars. Nitrogen is not affected by changes in temperature or humidity, so the tires keep their shape no matter how hot or cold the temperature gets.

- Bird droppings are known as guano, which is used as a fertilizer. Guano can contain as much as 10 percent nitrogen.

- The deepest scuba dive possible using compressed air is 510 feet (155 meters). At that depth, the water pressure is high enough to squeeze a person's chest to less than half its size.

To Find Out More

If you would like to learn more about nitrogen, check out these additional resources.

Books

Blashfield, Jean F. **Nitrogen.** Raintree/Steck-Vaughn, 1998.

Farndon, John. **Nitrogen.** Marshall Cavendish, 1998.

Fitzgerald, Karen. **The Story of Nitrogen.** Franklin Watts, 1997.

Organizations and Online Sites

Composting for Kids

http://aggie-horticulture. tamu.edu/sustainable/slides ets/kidscompost/cover.html

This site takes you through the steps needed to make your own fertilizer or compost that has a high nitrogen content.

Hey, It's Your Backyard

http://web.mit.edu/civenv/ K12Edu/activities/ gardens.html

Learn which conditions are best for breaking down compounds so that gases, such as nitrogen, are released. Experiment by setting up miniature compost piles in soda bottles and seeing which one releases the most gas.

See What Happens When You Get the Bends

http://www.seagrant.wisc. edu/madisonjason11/ experiment_bends.html

Use two soda bottles to see how nitrogen gas bubbles can cause the bends when a diver returns to the surface too quickly.

This Car Runs on Air

http://abcnews.go.com/ sections/science/DyeHard/ dye15.html

Read about a car that runs on liquid nitrogen.

Staying Cool in the Space Station

http://kids.msfc.nasa.gov/ news/2001/News- StationCool.asp

The sun can heat up one side of the Space Station to 250 degrees Fahrenheit (121 degrees C). Learn how ammonia is used to keep the astronauts inside cool.

Important Words

bacteria extremely small living things that help recycle nitrogen and turn it into a form useful to plants and animals

compound substance formed from the combination of two or more different elements

element building block of matter

matter stuff or material that makes up everything in the universe

nitrogen cycle nature's way of recycling nitrogen

protein compound that contains nitrogen

Index

(**Boldface** page numbers
    indicate illustrations.)

air, 6–8, 16, 17, 21
air pollution, 40–41
ammonia, 24–27, **25,** 30,
    35–36, 42
animals, 17, 21
bacteria, **18,** 19–21, 24, 42
"bends, the", 10
bloodstream, 8–10
breathing, 8, 17
bubbles, 10
burning, 14, **15**
Chile, 33, **34,** 35
compound, 19–21, 22,
    24, 31–32
compressed air, 6, 7, 43
diving, 5–10, 7
dynamite, 38
eardrums, 5–6
elements, 11–14, 16
energy, 23, 24
explosives, 32–36, **37**
fertilizers, 27–30, **29,** 43
gases, 6, 8–10

human body, 22–24
insulin, 24
lightning, 42
matter, 12–14
muscles, 22
nitrogen
    dangers, 31–41
    fun facts, 42–43
    what it is, 11–21
    why it's important,
        22–30
nitrogen cycle, 19–21, **20**
nitroglycerin, 36, 38
Nobel, Alfred, 38, **39**
oxygen, 14, **15**
plants, 17, 19, 21, 24, 27,
    27
pollution, 40–41
pressure, 5–10
proteins, 22–24
scuba divers, 6–10, 43
secret messages, 26
smog, 40–41
sodium nitrate, 33–34, 35
sugar, 24
World War I, 32–36

Meet the Author

Salvatore Tocci is a science writer who lives in East Hampton, New York, with his wife Patti. He was a high school biology and chemistry teacher for almost thirty years. His books include a high school chemistry textbook and an elementary school series that encourages students to perform experiments to learn about science. One of his favorite classroom demonstrations involved placing different things, such as a rubber ball and a rose, into liquid nitrogen.